M E N C I U S

Ancient Sages of China

MENCIUS

A Benevolent Saint for the Ages

By Xu Yuanxiang & Zhang Bing

| CHINA INTERCONTINENTAL PRESS |

CONTENTS

Introduction

Some 2,400 years ago in China, an ordinary man journeyed to the imperial palace where the king lived. This man was sufficiently bold to dare to rebuke the king for his mistakes. He fearlessly informed the king that if he was not qualified to rule, he should step down and make way for a better king. He even confidently advanced his own theory of government:"The people are the most important element

Front gate of the Mencius Mension.

in a state; next come the gods of land and grain; least of all is the ruler himself." This was undoubtedly the first Chinese expression of a theory of democratic administration. For an ordinary person to advance these progressive ideas and to criticize the behaviour of an all-powerful monarch was at this time to risk his life.

In the two millennia that have passed since this man lived, his thoughts and ideas have continued to have a major influence on the Chinese people. Even today, people can be regularly heard to quote the sayings of this man. This brave

Statue of Mencius
(372 BC-289 BC).

Statue of Socrates (469 BC-399 BC). Statue of Plato (427 BC-347 BC).

and intelligent person is known to history as Mencius—a benevolent saint for the ages.

In the 5th century BC, two of the greatest thinkers in the history of western civilization—Socrates and Plato—were born in the lands of the Greek archipelago. Amazingly, in the same century, two of the most renowned philosophers of eastern civilization—Confucius and Mencius—were born in the lands that are now known as China. Confucius is well known in the west, but most westerners are unfamiliar with Mencius and not many have even heard of him. In contrast,

Hometown of Mencius in Zou County in Shandong Province.

in China, Mencius is regarded with just as much respect and reverence as is Confucius.

Childhood

In an early morning in 372 BC, a baby was born to a noble family of the aristocratic name of "Meng," who had fallen on hard times. The most illustrious of the Meng ancestors had been appointed as prime minister of the State of Lu. However, when the baby was born, the family was in straitened circumstances and the whole family had to move from the prosperous capital to a small remote city so as to reduce their living expenses. Obviously, the birth of that baby added much to the financial burdens of the hard-pressed family.

The baby was named Ke, which had the same pronunciation as a Chinese character which means frustration. It was a custom with people in ancient China to use a character identical in pronunciation to a character they wanted to denote when naming a child. So while they didn't want to name their child "Frustration," they nevertheless wished him to remember the difficulties of the life the family was facing when the boy entered the world. They could never have predicted just how much frustration this baby would, in fact,

Ruins of the city walls of the State of Lu.

have to face during the course of his life; nor indeed could they possibly have foreseen that this baby would become one of the most famous figures in all of Chinese culture and civilization whose thoughts would influence countless generations of Chinese people.

Though the Meng family's circumstances at that time were not auspicious, they never neglected an age-old family tradition—that of providing their sons with a good education. Clever and warm-hearted, Mencius' mother

The temple was built to mark Mencius' mother who moved their home three times for a better neighborhood.

could never countenance the possibility that her son should grow up illiterate. Indeed when she was pregnant with Mencius, she often recited the famous *Book of Poetry* (Songs and Odes) to her belly eager to begin cultivating the literary sensibilities of the baby lying within.

New Year's painting created to tell the story of Mencius' mother who moved their home three times for a better neighborhood.

Today, practically all Chinese have heard the story of *Mencius's Mother Moves Three Times*.

The Meng's used to live on the outskirts of a city with a large graveyard where children without education always hung around. Influenced by these children, Mencius became one of them, regularly becoming involved in fistfights and various kinds of trouble. Concerned at the influence of these uncouth ruffians, Mencius' mother decided to move to a more respectable area of the city believing that this was in the best interests of her son's proper development. This was the first occasion the family moved.

A bazaar during the Warring States Period (475 BC-221 BC).

Eventually Mencius' mother chose as their new home a house beside a bazaar where people traded and negotiated and the peddler's cries carried on the fragrant summer air. Here, the ever-curious Mencius learned the tricks of the merchant, hawking and haggling and hoodwinking like the pedlars who festooned the market stalls. Merchants at that time enjoyed nothing like the status they have today—the once noble Meng family would have especially despised such a trade—so Mencius' mother was understandably concerned once again about the suitability of this environment for her son's growth and development. It was clearly time for the family to move again.

Their third home was in the neighborhood of a place called the Palace of Education—perhaps quite similar in its day to the position that Peking University holds in our own day. Namely. It was a place where intellectuals gathered and people of cultivation and breeding discussed the issues of the day. Mencius eagerly learned the importance of rites and

Ruins of the Palace of Education in Changyuan County, Henan Province. Confucius was said to have lectured in the palace.

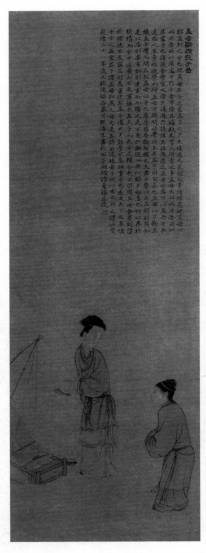

the imperatives of politeness and soon he was bowing and scraping whenever coming in and going out of even his own home. His mother sighed with great relief. At last she felt she had found the ideal environment for her son. The family settled down.

The ancient building of the Palace of Education was tranquil and solemn with often the only sound the restful drone of students reading aloud from their textbooks. Teachers and students were often to be seen practicing rites and when important festivals

Mencius' mother Taking Great Care of Teaching Her Son by Kang Tao (Qing Dynasty, 1616-1911).

Parents of Mencius.

came round each year, they would be celebrated with especially great ceremony. This was indeed a wonderful environment for a young man to grow up in. Mencius

Zou County of Shandong Province today.

soaked up the atmosphere and a great respect for, and indeed expertise in, the whole area of rites and ceremonies developed in this young man.

In that decade, it was not easy for a widowed mother and son to move home. In having to move home twice, we can see the mother's absolute determination to find a favorable environment for her son. Naturally a person's ultimate success depends largely on their own natural abilities and the application they could bring to their work but nevertheless it cannot be denied that for a young person the environment in which they grow up is an enormous factor in their development. The environment that his mother chose for the young Mencius to grow up in was a profound influence in his eventually becoming a master of Confucianism.

A Wandering Scholar

In the 5th century BC, Zou, where Mencius lived, was a very small state. Some 100 kilometers away to the north lay the State of Lu. Confucius had lived in the State of Lu

Tablets of Idioms in the Mencius Temple.
Left to right: Place Where Mother of Mencius Broke the Loom to Talk Mencius Over to Study Hard, Temple of Mother of Mencius Making Three Moves for Better Neighborhood, and Place Where Zisi Wrote His Middle Way.

Hall of Mencius in Zou County, Shandong Province.

In his late years Confucius (551 BC-479 BC) worked on classics and ran private schools.

one century before Mencius was born. Confucianism—the embodiment of the ideas of Confucius—was then in the ascendancy in the State of Lu and every spring and autumn, the followers of Confucius would hold a grand ceremony in the memorial temple. This occasion, because of the wonderful cultural atmosphere and the erudition of the scholars in attendance became an event of enormous

A portrait of Confucius by Ma Yuan (Song Dynasty, 960-1279).

importance and attracted people from far and near to attend.

When Mencius was a young man, he began, like Plato, to lead the life of a wandering scholar. He found himself very

attracted to the graceful and elegant style of Confucianism-
so much so that he decided to come to Confucius' hometown
to try to improve himself as a person.

The ceremony which involved offering sacrifices to
Confucius was the highlight of the celebrations. To young
Mencius, watching attentively, the idea that one's thoughts

Grand ritual held to worship Confucius.

Explanations on Benevolence in *Analects of Confucius*.

could influence later generations after one had passed from the world was most seductive. Mencius' devotion to Confucius was total. He once said, "Since humans have existed, there has been no greater man than Confucius." It was at that time that Mencius came to fully realize the road he wanted to take and the man he wanted to follow.

Thus, Mencius became a devoted follower of Confucianism and esteemed Confucius above all others. As he observed: "My hope is to learn from Confucius and follow his thoughts."

As we know the essence of Confucian thought lies in humanity and benevolence. Confucianism advocates benevolence above all else, but also love, duty, propriety, and wisdom. Confucius in his lifetime never fully expounded the reasons why, in fact, people should demonstrate these qualities of loving and benevolence. It was to be Mencius who would make this theoretical leap, pointing out that at birth, everyone is born intrinsically good.

Stone tablets of the Qing Dynasty (1616-1911) for Confucius and Mencius in Zou County in Shandong Province.

Halberd of the Warring States Period (475 BC-221 BC).

Departing radically from the concept of original sin, which is an important doctrine of Christianity, Mencius believed that everyone was born morally good. He illustrated his point with the following example: when someone falls into a river, natural human instinct is to try to save the person in trouble. Mencius' theory of intrinsic human goodness was not only a profound development of Confucius' thoughts on humanity, but it also destined him to a lonely road of dissent and opposition for he found that his ideas were fundamentally out of step with the prevailing notions of the day.

"Benevolent Kingship" Vs "Hegemony"

Mencius lived in an era known to history as the Warring States Period (475 BC-221 BC). What had been the dominant power, the State of Zhou, had already broken up and what followed was a period of internecine struggle for hegemony between the seven most powerful remaining states.

Farmers in Jinan, Shandong Province, have invested in construction of the Warring States (475 BC-221 BC) Movie Town. The new tourist spot is magnetic to Chinese and foreign visitors.

It was a time of almost constant war, broken intermittently by shaky strategic ceasefires, little more in fact than pauses. According to the historical records during this period, 125 wars took place and very few years did not witness major conflict. One illustration from that cruel period is enough to give one a hint of the ruthlessness and barbarity of the times: In a battle between the State of Qin and the State of Zhao, 300,000 captives were massacred by the Qin forces and the blood of the dead flowed in a river so large that a small wooden boat could sail upon it.

As is always true, constant warfare caused untold suffering for the ordinary people in the lands where the fighting took place. The State of Song, for example, was besieged for a number of months. Their food stores greatly depleted, in

Congtai Terrace built 2,300 years ago for Duke Wuling of the Zhao State. Located in the northeastern part of Handan, Hebei Province, it was used for watching military parades and theatrical performance.

time the people were reduced to cannibalism; to eating their own children just to survive. As if this was not hellish enough, it is said that the meat was often cooked using the corpses of the dead as fuel. Such savagery is the inevitable consequence of the hardships caused by war.

The seven most powerful states at that time—Qi, Chu, Yan, Han, Zhao, Wei and Qin which were known as the "Seven Great Powers" during the Warring States Period (475 BC-221 BC) were all equally determined to overcome their enemies and emerge as the ultimate victor. The battlefield was the only medium they saw as being useful in the achievement of this bloody ambition.

All the chaos, cruelty and suffering that accompany human conflict were to be found in abundance during these wars. Mencius looked on aghast at the terrible crimes against humanity he saw being committed day after day:"These kings and generals seek to expand their power and territory using the coin of those who die for them in battle. They have reduced the land to barbarism; they have caused people to eat human flesh. They deserve a punishment that goes beyond death." The bitterness of Mencius' denunciation was borne of firsthand experience: he had lived through and seen with his own eyes the ravages that war wreaks on the land

Great Wall

Defensive walls were first built during the Warring States Period (475 BC-221 BC). In the Qin Dynasty (221 BC-206 BC), they were connected and expanded into the Great Wall extending to some 10,000 *li* or 5,000 km. Large-scale reconstruction was carried out during the Han (206 BC-220 AD) and Ming (1368-1644) Dynasties.

War horses and horse-drawn carts were buried in the pit. During the Warring States Period (475 BC-221 BC), Sanmenxia in Henan Province was the site of the Hao State, and Hao was eliminated by the Qin State.

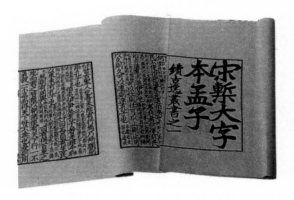

Song Dynasty (960-1279) edition of *Mencius*.

and the people. He determined to find a better way: a way focused more on benevolent kingship and less on hegemony and dominance.

What is the difference between "benevolent kingship" and "hegemony?" Mencius, along with many other contemporary commentators, advocated the unification of the country. The existing emphasis on "hegemony" stressed military power and economic vitality as the means by which one power could rise above the others and thus achieve unification in a Darwinian struggle: the "fittest" and "strongest" would emerge victorious. Confucianists, like Mencius, advocated "benevolent kingship": an alternative approach where the loyalty and support of the people would be won not through overwhelming physical power but by means of a benevolent and compassionate administration as the vehicle to bring about national unification.

Mencius and King of Wei

The bitter military struggles between the various Chinese states provided a stage for a number of notable people, as kings eagerly gathered around themselves talented individuals who could contribute towards the ultimate goal of military victory and national hegemony. Thus, a diplomatic, political class came into being, a group of thinkers whose area of expertise was politics and whose aspiration was to turn their political ideals into reality by becoming involved in the administration of the various states.

As each king frantically thirsted for ultimate power, talented diplomats were always in demand and could move between the various states with relative freedom. This made for a very fluid environment for the transmission of various ideas and theories of government and many different schools of thought gained widespread popularity. Thus, the Warring States period (475 BC-221 BC) provided the ideal soil for

Prince Xinlingjun of the State of Wei Paying Visit to Wise Man Hou Ying by
Wu Li (Qing Dynasty, 1616-1911).

Gate to Mencius Mansion.

the growth of various academic, militaristic, religious and legalistic schools of thought, some of the most notable of which were Confucianism, Taoism, Military strategy, Legalism, and Geomancy.

This turbulent era produced a whole spectrum of philosophical speculation. Some focused only on physical reality—how best a battle could be won; how best a soldier could be prepared. Others sought to escape from reality and ponder more metaphysical notions of existence and humanity. Many brave men did not fear to articulate their ideas publicly despite potentially fatal consequences. Mencius was perhaps the most notable of this group. He consistently criticized the prevailing militaristic, hegemonic orthodoxy of the day, advocating instead a road leading to peace: to a lessening of the terrible sufferings that the common people had to face every day of these difficult times. In 320 BC, his reputation as a learned and profound thinker well established, Mencius eventually got the chance to put his ideals into some form of practice in the State of Wei.

In 341 BC, the State of Wei had attacked the State of Zhao, which in turn appealed for assistance from the State of Qi—a major power in the east. The Qi sent out an expeditionary army to attack the capital of Wei so as to relieve the pressure on Zhao. In a battle with Qi, the forces of Wei, commanded by General Pangjuan, were encircled by the Qi forces in a place called Maling. Over 100,000 Wei soldiers were massacred, among them General Pangjuan. The Wei prince, Shen, was also captured, and Maling Battle took its place as one of the bloodiest and most significant battles in ancient Chinese history.

Daliangmen City Wall Tower in Kaifeng, Henan Province.

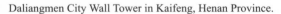

Part of the bronze pot of the Warring States Period (475 BC-221 BC) which has patterns telling battles during the Warring States Period.

Liang Hui Wang, the King of Wei, faced with the overwhelming dangers posed by the Qi armies, had no choice but to move his capital south to nearby Daliang, what is today Kaifeng in Henan Province. Liang Hui Wang was at this time very close to total despair, but he never lost his determination to rejuvenate his State. In 320 BC, with the promise of munificent working conditions, he made a great

A portrait of middle-aged Mencius.

effort to recruit extremely talented individuals to help with the rebuilding of his State. On learning this, Mencius who was 53 years old at that time thought it was an excellent opportunity and decided to go to the Wei capital, Daliang (present-day Kaifeng) to try his luck. This was the background to the fateful meeting between king and thinker with which our story began.

Mencius arrived in Wei and, in their first meeting, immediately quarreled with Liang Hui Wang. Liang Hui Wang was a practical and somewhat blunt man and asked straight out what benefits such an old person who had travelled such a long way could possibly bring to the State of Wei. He expected that Mencius would try to impress him with similar policies he had heard a thousand times before: policies designed to make the country rich and the army more powerful.

Mencius said:"As the leader of the country, you seek the

Doors of the Mencius Mansion.

best for yourself personally. It follows that your high-ranking officials and your people will adopt the same attitude. It is very dangerous for a country if everyone seeks benefits only for himself. As the leader of the country, you should advocate benevolence and righteousness. This is the only way forward for your State."

Unfortunately King Liang Hui Wang at that time was in very poor health. He was in fact close to death and thus sought short-term measures to remedy the emergency his

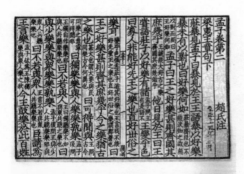

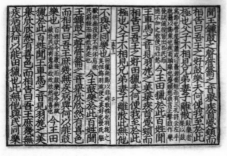

State faced. He had no time for the long-term prescription that Mencius was offering him. He saw Mencius' ideas as pie-in-the-sky theories and dismissed them as useless. Did the king, in fact, have a point? Was the knowledgeable Mencius merely a

Mencius Goes to See King Hui Wang of the Liang State.

pedant, preaching theories that had no practical application to the reality of worldly affairs?

Mencius advocated Confucian benevolence: he dismissed Liang Hui Wang's eagerness to find more practically effective solutions. He elaborated in detail why benevolence and not some utilitarian philosophy was the way in which the State could be saved. According to Mencius, if everyone focused on their own self-interest, conflict and confrontation would inevitably occur and the country could well descend into chaos. If, on the other hand, the king promoted benevolence and righteousness, he would win the willing support of the people, the most important prerequisite for constructive

Sacrificial objects of the Mencius Mansion.

Stone arch of the Temple of Mencius.

redevelopment.

As is the case with many great philosophers, the brilliance of the ideas of Mencius were too advanced for his own day and had to await a future time to be implemented. The Warring States period (475 BC-221 BC) was an era too blinded by blood and conflict to recognize the purity of the flame of Mencius' theories. What would Liang Hui Wang, so anxious to alleviate his State's desperate situation, decide in relation to the interesting ideas of this philosopher/sage?

Liang Hui Wang, already at that time in his 70s, admired Mencius' political ideas. However, the Wei State was facing imminent extinction: they stood weakened in the midst of the three major powers of the day, the States of Qin, Chu and Qi, and given the rapaciousness of the times, had to expect one of them to attack sooner rather than later. The king needed effective policies to deal with this crisis and not an overall philosophical theory for administering a state. If no action was taken, there soon might not even be a state.

Seeing King Liang Hui's skepticism, Mencius then decided to try another tack with the aged king. He spoke about the bright future a benevolent administration could hope to enjoy:"Perhaps Your Majesty thinks my ideas are somewhat impractical, but this is certainly not the case. Those major military powers like Qin and Chu expend all their energies on mobilizing and attacking—their people must be ready to go to war at any moment. How can such a nation tend their crops and nurture their families? They are pushing their people inexorably into an abyss of suffering. If you adopt a

Ancient battle carts unearthed from the Linzi Ancient Carts Museum of Shandong Province.

benevolent policy, you will have standardized laws, a strong economy, a well-educated and ambitious people. If, at that time, you decide the moment demands an assault on another State, none shall be able to resist your combined power at that time."

The very essence of benevolent administration was to

Mencius—A Benevolent Saint for the Ages

Ancient trees in the Temple of Mencius.

implement the concept of benevolence in the realm of politics and allow a State to reach its political goals by means of the force of ethical righteousness.

Mencius placed great emphasis on the role national morale could play. He summarized the lessons of the dynasties of Xia (21st century BC-16th century BC), Shang (16th century BC-11th century BC) and Zhou (11th century BC-256 BC) in acquiring, and then subsequently, letting slip, power and

Lingxing Gate of the Temple of Mencius.

Stone tablet in the Tomb of Mencius' Mother.

hegemony and said that the reason why King Jie and Zhou lost their states was that they lost the mandate of the people. There were ways to gain the trust and win the hearts of the people, but the central priority should always be to give the people what they expected and not what was obviously inimical to their wellbeing. In essence it is a rephrasing of Confucius' famous maxim: "Don't do to others what you do not want others to do to you." The essential humanity of such a world view made it a powerfully benevolent tool when used in the realm of administration and government.

Eventually Mencius determined efforts to promote the benefits of benevolent administration to the aged king proved unsuccessful. True, Liang Hui Wang was moved

Wooden Nuange container for "four treasures of the study" (writing brush, ink stick, ink slab and paper) and seals in the Datang Hall of Mencius Mansion.

by the passion and persuasiveness of this great thinker. The two finally joined hands, but unfortunately this meeting of minds, which could potentially have borne great and peaceful fruit, was to be to no avail. The king's health failed at last and so Mencius' hopes for seeing a nation administered by the guiding light of benevolent compassion died with the old king.

Mencius and King of Qi

In 318 BC, Liang Xiang Wang, Liang Hui Wang's son, succeeded to the throne. Mencius decided to begin again and elaborate his political ideas to this young king, but he saw little hope of any success.

The new king met Mencius with his beautiful array of concubines beside him. Though the State was facing imminent invasion: enemy troops were mustering on the border and its territory was being gradually diminished day by day, the king cared little and worried less. The new king was somewhat of a playboy. Mencius, in despair, saw that he would be wasting his breath explaining his ideas to this imbecile wastrel and so determined to leave the State of Wei once and for all.

Qi Great Wall
During the Warring States Period (475 BC-221 BC), the Qi State (within present-day Shandong Province), built defensive walls on its border with the Lu State. The Zhangqiu section of the Qi Wall in Ji'nan of Shandong Province was the oldest of defensive walls built in China. According to historical records, construction of the Qi Wall began in 404 BC and was completed under the reign of King Qi Xuan Wang.

In the autumn in 318 BC, a disappointed Mencius left Wei. Standing on the border of the State, his sad eyes beheld a world full of war and suffering. Mencius felt utterly alone and in darkness. Where now could he go to try to realize the dreams in his heart?

He turned his eyes to the State of Qi in the east.

According to the *Chronicles of The Grand Historian*, Zibo in Shandong Province, the old capital of the State of Qi, had a population of 70,000 households. During the period of the warring states, the State of Qi, with a population of some 70,000 households, was among the preeminent powers of the day and could rapidly mobilize some 210,000 soldiers. It was an awesome military power.

In 318 BC, a major turning point in Chinese history occurred: five States located in the centre of what is now China—namely, the states of Han, Zhao, Wei, Yan and

Sewer of the capital of the Qi State.

Chu joined forces to launch an assault on the most powerful state, the Qin in an attempt to annihilate them. Their efforts were in vain, however, as the resilient Qin armies emerged victorious in a major battle at Hanguguan. This triumph set in train a process where those five states, after their unsuccessful gambit, steadily declined in power and influence, leaving two main "superpowers" to dispute overall hegemony. These were the Qin in the west and the Qi in the east.

Despite this preeminence, the King of Qi was in apprehensive mood. He saw that the Qin victory over the five allied states had tipped the balance of power in their favour. If the Qin united the five defeated states to form one ultra-powerful State in the Central Plains, the State of Qi could never hope to match them. Qi Xuan Wang, the king of Qi at this time, realized that only political reform and not military confrontation could strengthen his state's position and enable the Qi to avoid the terrible fate of the five defeated States. In line with his newly acquired aspirations towards reform, the first thing he did was to seek talented and visionary people who could assist him in governing the country in accordance with these new ideas.

Jixia Palace of Education in the state of Qi was the place

the King looked to recruit the people he needed. Like an Ivy League university in today's world, there were gathered at Suxia more than 1,000 outstanding intellectuals, who were provided with the very best living environment and amenities by the government of Qi in order that they could devote all possible efforts to coming up with ways to better and more efficiently administer the state.

In 318 BC, Mencius moved to Suxia Palace of Education. He had been pondering for some time the ultimate failure

Ruins of the Jixia Palace of Education in Lingzi.

Wood carvings in the Tomb of Mencius' Mother.

of his efforts to influence the Wei administration. He concluded that it was not really a propitious time for the Wei, beset as they were by crisis, to introduce, what was at the time a daring, almost revolutionary, new attitude towards government. Looking at the prosperous and strong State of Qi, Mencius felt much more hopeful that here he might achieve success..

After some time, King Qi Xuan Wang met and talked with Mencius. In the luxury palace of the State of Qi, the king asked him a very strange historic question, "Can you tell me how it was that Qi Huan Gong and Jin Wen Gong managed to become great rulers during the Spring and Autumn Period (770 BC-476 BC)?" Qi Xuan Wang, under cover of testing

Mencius' knowledge of history, was in fact revealing his preoccupation with ultimate power for himself and his State. He hoped Mencius' reply would give the Confucian seal of approval to his own efforts to expand the power of the Qi state. Mencius at this time was widely recognised as perhaps the foremost representative of the Confucian school.

Mencius gave an unexpected reply. He said that he never spoke, or would ever speak, about ways to achieve ultimate power and hegemony. What was Mencius doing? Here he was facing a great opportunity to convert one of the most powerful rulers in the land to his benevolent philosophy and he was straight away giving the king a negative answer.

Mencius continued in a vein that cannot have been

Wood pillars in the Tomb of Mencius' Mother.

New Year Painting: *Qi Huan Gong Becoming a Powerful Ruler Because of Importance He Gave to Talent Ning Qi.*

pleasing to the king's ears. He stated that rulers like Qi Huan Gong and Jin Wen Gong were the very antithesis of what a good and benevolent king should be. As he pointed out:"If your prime minister rebels, he is a sinner to you. The rest may be deduced by analogy. If you want to follow the example of Qi Huang Gong and Jin Wen Gong, I am afraid you will be endangering your throne. Why? Both King Qihuan and Jianwen overthrew others, and if you imitate them, you will set a dangerous precedent for your subordinates."

The fearless Confucian offered the opinion that it was not necessary for Qi Xuan Wang to learn anything from Qi Huan Gong or Jin Wen Gong if he really wanted to know how to lead the country well. These two merely desired power as the ultimate end in itself. They had no broader vision. But to rule a country well, Mencius continued, it would be more profitable to properly investigate the true meaning of 'kingship' because this knowledge could really help a ruler to become a true king of his people.

Jin Wen Gong Staging a Comeback by Li Tang (Southern Song Dynasty, 1127-1279).

Qi Xuan Wang asked how this concept and practice of "kingship" could be used to unite the lands. Mencius answered:"If a king shares the worries and concerns of his subjects and makes policies that enable them to live and work in peace and contentment, there is no force in existence that can stop him uniting the world."

Despite Mencius' passionate advocacy, Qi Xuan Wang was not convinced and doubted his capacity to effectively implement this concept of "kingship" in the real world. Qi Xuan Wang told the wise Confucian that it was neither

Coiling Dragon Yellow Jade Pendant (23.6 cm long) unearthed from the ruins of the Zhongshan State of the Warring States Period (475 BC-221 BC).

practical nor possible to implement such dramatic changes at that time. Undaunted Mencius contradicted the king, pointing out that yes, it was indeed possible to implement these changes now for the very reason that the king bore a strong love for his people. The puzzled king asked Mencius how he could possibly know this.

The sage replied: "I heard from one of your ministers that the Qi had constructed a huge

Mencius Answering Questions by the King of Qi.

bell and wanted to sacrifice an ox to it. When you saw the ox was shivering with dread, you took pity on the beast and asked that it be replaced with a goat." Qi Xuan Wang smiled and confirmed that this had in fact occurred.

Datang Hall of the Mencius Mansion.

Mencius went on:"You are clearly a benevolent and sympathetic man. If you could utilize your feelings; your very nature, in the ruling of the country, you would without doubt be successful."

These words echo, even to our own ears today, with the wisdom and eloquence of Mencius. Qi Xuan Wang was very impressed with the ideas of his learned adviser and he told

Path leading to the Tomb of Mencius and his offspring.

Tombs of parents of Mencius.

Mencius "There is a sentence in the great Book of Poetry, which reads 'I can guess the worries of others.' I see now that it was written for you, Wise Sage. You know me well. But tell me in more detail how I can utilize this concept of 'kingship': how I can utilize my benevolent nature to become a true king of the world."

Mencius answered with a revealing example: "It is not possible for a person to carry Taishan Mountain on his back and cross the Northern Seas, but it is absolutely possible for him to pluck a twig from a low hanging tree." The point Mencius was making was that the issue was not the means by which the concept of 'kingship' could be implemented but rather whether the will and the desire to implement these policies existed. The problem was not how it could be done but whether the king was willing to try.

It was in this way that Mencius began to win over the previously skeptical king to his point of view.

However, Qi Xuan Wang, who still after all had been brought up and educated in an era which taught that 'power comes from victory in war', remained unclear about many aspects of Mencius' kingship ideas, which stressed an overwhelming reliance on benevolence and not force of arms to govern the country. He urged Mencius to tell him more.

Mencius' failure in the state of Wei had taught him a lot and this time he steered away from vague and general theories, and focused instead on the economic benefits a benevolent administration would bring to the ruler and the people of the State.

Mencius pointed out to the king that the most important area in which benevolent administration would bring benefits was in the realm of "permanent assets": essentially the land—the most basic resource in feudal, and indeed in modern, times. Mencius essential theory in this regard was that farmers should own the land.

According to Mencius, endowed with appreciating permanent assets, people would settle down and lead stable productive lives. Without permanent assets, people's existence would always be precarious and unpredictable. Thus the land would always be at risk from outbursts of rebellion and even revolution.

However, Mencius' egalitarian theory of private land ownership was an absolute bridge too far in the eyes of Qi Xuan Wang. At that time and for many centuries to come, kings considered all the land of their realm their own private property and all the people living thereon their slaves. Mencius' theories had understandable appeal among the

Steles in the Temple of Mencius.

common people and Qi Xuan Wang thus had to show him a certain measure of respect, but the idea of a king granting ownership of land to his people was a completely ridiculous idea in the king's view. The king remained essentially an unreconstructed power-hungry ruler of the old school but he did recognise the possibilities of adopting some appearance of being a benevolent and compassionate ruler, the better, he slyly thought, to achieve his political and military dreams of ultimate power.

In the second year after Mencius' arrival in the state of Qi, the king of the neighboring Yan State to the north died and his son, Yi Wang, not without strong opposition, succeeded. Qi Xuan Wang took advantage of the situation and invaded the lands of Yan.

The Qi troops quickly conquered a dozen Yan cities, aided in no small part by the civil war raging in the troubled State. Qi Xuan Wang found himself caught on the horns of a dilemma at that time. On the one hand he was pleased and proud of the success of his military forces but on the other hand, the lack of public support for his adventurous Yan invasions was a great source of worry. Mulling over this problem, his thoughts turned once more to the persuasive and passionate

Mencius—A Benevolent Saint for the Ages

Tombs of Four Kings of the Qi State, located at Lingzi, Shandong Province. Legend has it that they are tombs of Qi Wei Wang, Qi Xuan Wang, Qi Min Wang and Qi Xiang Wang (here Wang means king in English).

War Horse Burying Pit of the Qi State, located at Zibo of Shandong Province. It reminds people of the incessant wars then.

counselor, Mencius, a man and a thinker who enjoyed uncommon prestige and popularity among the common people.

He summoned Mencius and told him:"Some suggest I quit my invasion at this point; others argue I should press ahead and subjugate the whole State. If I choose the latter course of action it will take no more than two months because of our overwhelming military superiority. What then should I do? Will conquering this State cause the gods to rain down disasters on my head? What do you advise?"

Mencius replied, "If the people of Yan wish it, you must press on; If they do not wish it, then desist. Right now the Yan people shower your troops with food, wine and good wishes because they see in you the opportunity for a return to normality and peace. If the situation should worsen however, they will call for others to rescue them from you."

The Qi army, in the end, rampaged through the Yan territory, tyrannizing the people and plundering their resources. A great resistance movement sprung up among the downtrodden Yan. Again the delicate balance of power had been upset and other powers resolved to send forces to the state of Yan to help them in their struggle against the tyrannous Qi. Faced with such considerable 'international' pressure and condemnation, Qi Xuan Wang had no option but to return the ten cities his forces had occupied.

From the Qi capital, Linzi, Mencius watched sadly as batallion after batallion of soldiers marched to the front and company after company of injured came the other way moving towards the rear. The great and cruel games of war were in progress once again. The Masters of War had sounded the fateful trumpets once more and the masses were again forced to march to their pointless doom. Weeping widows, dismembered bodies, fields of bloodied corpses filled the land and Mencius' heart could not bear it any longer.

He went to the court once more and fearlessly declared to Qi Xuan Wang that both Jie—the last emperor of the Xia Dyasty (21st century BC-16th century BC) and Zhou—the last emperor of the Shang Dynasty (16th century BC-11th century BC) had lost their grip on power in exactly this fashion—they lost the support of the people just as the king was now doing with his cruel war. "The people are the most important element in a state; next are the gods of the land and grain; least of all is the ruler himself. A real emperor must win the support of the people and a prince must win the heart of the emperor. If the prince endangers his country, he must give way and allow more outstanding candidates to

Statue of Mencius in the Temple of Mencius in Zou County, Shandong Province.

Mencius—A Benevolent Saint for the Ages

The barracks believed to be of the Qi State period were found in Zihe Town,
Zichuan of Shandong Province. Built along a mountain slope, the barracks were
composed of more than 100 rooms.

take his place."

Confucianism is essentially a human-oriented philosophy and for Mencius this aspect of his beliefs ruled supreme over all others. During the turbulent Warring States Period (475 BC-221 BC) in particular, the prevailing political theorists of the day all advocated the waging of war and military might as the only path to glory and power. Confucianism remained steadfast and consistently swam against the tides of the moment to advocate the establishment of a stable and peaceful society centred on the welfare of the people of the land.

What impresses us most today is Mencius' utter fearlessness in expounding his theories and denouncing those he saw as evil and wrong. He risked his life speaking out for what he believed. In those days a king had godlike, absolute power and could order the deaths of anyone on the slightest whim. Mencius was fully aware of this but nevertheless remained undaunted and raised his voice without fear to point out the absolute folly and evil of the king's misguided policies.

As Mencius enjoyed very high prestige in almost every state in the land, Qi Xuan Wang did not dare to kill him; it would have made his position vis-a-vis the other states

Mencius Mansion.

nigh on impossible. However, Mencius' students were
nevertheless enormously fearful about what fate would befall
their courageous master. Mencius elaborated his idea of life
and death as follows:"I desire Fish but I also desire bear's

Mencius—A Benevolent Saint for the Ages

Mencius Giving Lectures.

A portrait of Mencius.

paw. If I choose the bear's paw I must relinquish the fish since I cannot have both. Similarly I desire Life but also righteousness. So, if I cannot have both I will choose righteousness and relinquish life."

Mencius' Spirit

In 312 BC when he was 62 years old, Mencius gave up the patronage of Qi Xuan Wang and left the state of Qi.

Again Mencius had tasted failure in protracted dealings with a ruling monarch. One must attribute a large portion of the reason for the great man's failure to the spirit of

the times. This time
of conflict was one
where the ears of
rulers were closed to
all but the aggressive
counsel of war and
acquisition. There
was no place in those
days for enlightened
benevolence and
compassion.

As the slanting
rays of the sun shone
wanly on his stooped
figure, accompanied
by his many disciples
and students, Mencius
left the lands of Qi
and headed for his
hometown. He settled

Xiaoxiang Bamboos in Wind
by Li Fangying (Qing Dynasty,
1616-1911).

Horizontal board inscribed by Qing Emperor Yongzheng (1678-1735), which is kept in the Datang Hall of the Mencius Mansion.

in the land where he had been born and grown up and where his dear mother now rested in the earth. Mencius set up a school there and continued to spread his theories of benevolent administration, determined to sow seeds that might blossom when the times were more propitious. Mencius provided people with a living example of how an upright person should live his life no matter how many frustrations and how much heartbreak that life might contain.

From a historical perspective, the most important thing about Mencius was his great perseverance and faith in the face of countless setbacks and disappointments. His ideas about the relationship between justice and the common good are lessons that echo down through the ages to our own time. He teaches us the importance of life but beyond that something even more important than life: a belief, a spirit

Tomb of Mencius in Zou County of Shandong Province.

Mencius—A Benevolent Saint for the Ages

that makes our lives meaningful.

Mencius was the very epitome of benevolence and compassion. He advocated the ideal of "the truly great man,": one whom no amount of money and power could corrupt; whom no poverty or hardship could dispirit; whom no tyrant or oppressor could silence. This conception of

Mencius Academy of Study in Zou County of Shandong Province.

More than 1,000 people played erhu (two-stringed musical instrument) together in Zou County of Shandong Province, hometown of Mencius, in the evening of April 27, 2006.

the right way to live one's life has had a profound influence on Chinese civilization and many of the great minds of successive eras have done their best to live up to these ideals.

Mencius' life and teachings form an important link with his great predecessor, Confucius and are an important link in the universal chain that forms the spirit of the Chinese nation. From very ancient times right down to the present day, idealistic people, common people included, have been inspired by this spirit which has blended with the very lifeblood of the nation.

In 289 BC, Mencius died peacefully in his hometown at the age of 82. A great temple was constructed after the model of the Confucian Temple in Zou, to honour the great man. Mencius, in the minds of the Chinese people, ranks second only to Confucius in terms of reverence, honour and devotion.

For thousands of years, idealistic people from China and beyond have absorbed the teachings of this great sage and will ensure his wisdom continues to resound to the heavens. One of his observations is especially apposite for our own times. It is a fitting way to end:"When Heaven is about to place great responsibility on a man, it always first frustrates his spirit and will, exhausts his muscles and bones, exposes him to starvation and poverty, plagues him with misfortune and setbacks so as to stimulate his spirit, toughen his nature and enhance his abilities."

图书在版编目（CIP）数据

亚圣——孟子：英文/徐远翔，张兵著；汉佳，王国振译.
北京：五洲传播出版社，2006.12（2008.1重印）
ISBN 978-7-5085-1039-2

Ⅰ.亚... Ⅱ.①徐...②张...③汉...④王... Ⅲ.孟轲（前372～前289）
－思想评论－英文 Ⅳ.B222.55

中国版本图书馆CIP数据核字（2008）第009028号

顾　　问：冷成金
作　　者：徐远翔　张　兵
译　　者：汉　佳　王国振
图片提供：中国新闻图片网
　　　　　国务院新闻办公室图片库
　　　　　北大光之桥图片工作室　等
策划编辑：荆孝敏
责任编辑：王　莉
设计总监：闫志杰
设计制作：刘　娜

亚圣——孟子

出版发行：五洲传播出版社
地址：中国北京市海淀区北小马厂6号华天大厦24层
邮编：100038
电话：010-58891281
传真：010-58891281
印刷：北京画中画印刷有限公司
开本：32开
印张：3
印数：3001-5000
版次：2007年1月第1版　2008年1月第2次印刷
书号：ISBN 978-7-5085-1039-2
定价：43.00元

Mencius—A Benevolent Saint for the Ages

Confucius and Mencius are known in the Chinese history as the two greatest sages. In the two millennia that have passed since Mencius lived, his thoughts and ideas have continued to have a major influence on the Chinese people. Even today, people can be regularly heard to quote the sayings of this man....

ISBN 978-7-5085-1039-2

9 787508 510392 >

RMB 43.00 Yuan